THE HABIT BLUEPRINT

15 SIMPLE STEPS TO
TRANSFORM YOUR LIFE

D0824000

PATRIK EDBLAD
www.Patrikedblad.com

Publishing services provided by:

ISBN-13: 978-1540451781
ISBN-10: 154045178X

Disclaimer:

Please note that this book is for entertainment purposes only. The views expressed are those of the author alone, and should not be taken as expert instruction or commands. The reader is responsible for his or her actions.

What Others Are Saying About "The Habit Blueprint"

"Many people want to improve their habits, but don't know how to get started. Fortunately, Patrik Edblad provides a simple step-by-step solution for starting (and sticking) to a new routine. It's the perfect resource for anyone who struggles to create lasting change in their lives." — **Steve Scott, bestselling author of** *Habit Stacking: 97 Small Life Changes That Take Five Minutes or Less*

"Patrik Edblad shows you how to create unbreakable habits without breaking a sweat. When you learn these skills, you'll have the secret sauce to finally follow through on your goals without giving up or getting frustrated. A must-read if you're serious about sustaining habits." — **Barrie Davenport, bestselling author of** *Sticky Habits: How to Achieve Your Goals without Quitting and Create Unbreakable Habits Starting with Five Minutes a Day*

"I've personally witnessed Patrik lead hundreds of people to complete and total life transformations. This powerful book captures every one of Patrik's habit systems and tricks. With this book in your hand, you will create as many new habits as you can imagine." — **Tony Stubblebine, founder of award-winning habit tracking app Coach.me**

Your Free Gifts

As a way of saying thank you for your purchase, I'd like to offer you two complimentary gifts:

1. *The Habit Blueprint Workbook.* We'll be covering a lot of powerful strategies in this book. To make it as easy as possible for you to implement them into your life, I've created a step-by-step checklist you can use every time you get started with a new habit. This resource takes you through all the steps outlined in this book one by one, so you can make sure you put all the strategies to work for you as efficiently as possible.

Go Here to Grab *The Habit Blueprint Workbook*:

www.patrikedblad.com/the-habit-blueprint-book-bonuses

2. *The Science of Willpower: Proven Strategies to Beat Procrastination & Get Big Things Done.* This e-book will show you:

- Why self-control is so important;
- How willpower works like a muscle;
- Why you should manage your energy, not your time;
- The physiology of self-control;
- Five cornerstone habits of willpower;
- Five powerful tactics to increase your willpower;
- And much more.

Go Here to Grab *The Science of Willpower: Proven Strategies to Beat Procrastination & Get Big Things Done*:

www.patrikedblad.com/the-habit-blueprint-book-bonuses

Get The Good Life Blueprint Audio Series
FOR FREE

If you enjoy listening to audiobooks, I have great news for you! You can get the entire audio version of *The Good Life Blueprint Series* for FREE by signing up for a 30-day Audible trial.

Go here to get started:

https://geni.us/Edblad-TGLB-Audible

Table of Contents

Introduction

According to research from Duke University[1], somewhere around 40 percent of the actions people perform every day aren't due to decision making but habits.

Take a moment to reflect on what that means. Almost half of the things you do on a given day aren't the result of conscious decisions but behaviors that you have repeated so many times they have become more or less automatic. You no longer think about them, you just do them.

Imagine what it would mean to you if you could find a way to change this 40 percent of actions so that you got them to work for you in every area of your life. What would it mean for your health? Your finances? Your relationships? Your personal growth?

This is why I absolutely love the topic of habits. It's also why I think understanding the mechanics of human behavior is a crucial skill in life. Because when we understand human behavior, it enables us to create our habits, which then create us. Almost every area of life reflects our daily habits:

- How in shape you are is a result of your habits.
- How productive you are is a result of your habits.
- How educated you are is a result of your habits.
- How much money you have is a result of your habits.
- How good your relationships are is a result of your habits.
- How happy you are is a result of your habits.

When we don't have a proper understanding of how habits work, we try to force our way to change by sheer will and usually end up at square one within a matter of months (or days). What's worse, each time we fail, we lose a little bit more confidence and get more and more discouraged until learned helplessness sets in.

If you're at the point where new-year resolutions have become something you keep just for the sake of keeping resolutions, rather than actually going after them, you know exactly what I mean. And you're not alone. About 92 percent of people fail at their resolutions every year[2].

But that also means 8 percent actually follow through on their goals. And contrary to what you might expect, these people are no different from you. They don't possess superhuman levels of self-control and some innate drive that makes them unbeatable.

What separates the habitual achievers from the rest is simply a system they've found to work for them that they use over and over again to create the change they want in all areas of life.

The only thing that stands between you and your most desired goals is really nothing more than a systematic, proven strategy you can use to make them a reality.

This book contains that strategy.

In the next couple of chapters, you'll be guided through a series of scientifically proven techniques for creating habits. Everything will be laid out with very simple, step-by-step explanations and actions based on the latest and best research regarding behavior change.

Sound good? Let's do this thing!

How to Use This Book

There are two ways you can read this book: passively or actively. Passively means you consume the material, getting a bit of entertainment and learn some new stuff. Reading actively, on the other hand, means you engage with the material, think about how the strategies outlined relate to you, and most importantly, take action on what you learn.

This book contains all the strategies you need to establish new habits and create massive change in your life. But that will only happen if you actually put the tactics to use.

So don't confuse motion with action. Don't settle for just reading passively, nodding along as you go, thinking, "yeah, I should probably do that." Ideas are worthless without execution. So make a commitment right now to experiment with what you're learning. Doing this will not be as comfortable as just reading, but it will make all the difference in how much value you get out of this book.

Since you're the biggest expert in the world on your behavior (and since you likely don't have access to a team of researchers who could do it for you), I encourage you to take on the roles of both scientist and subject from this point forward.

Let life become your experiment and the world your lab.

If you can successfully adopt this "scientist and subject" mindset[3], you'll dramatically increase your chances of creating whatever change you want in your life. Why? Because now, you cannot fail.

Where most people see setbacks as proof of their incompetence and as a sign that they should quit, you'll see valuable data and feedback you can use for your next attempt. Instead of seeing your change as something you have to do, you'll view it as something you want to do. Instead of getting discouraged, you'll get curious. Instead of quitting, you'll persistently refine your approach until you've found a way that works for you.

Sounds good? Are you ready to experiment? Awesome!

I recommend you start by reading through the entire book first. Doing this will give you a good idea of all the strategies and allow your brain to start working on how you could most effectively put them to use. Then download The Habit Blueprint Workbook, pick a habit you'd like to create, and get to work!

Let's get to it!

The Habit Loop

We'll begin by examining how habits work. One very helpful framework for doing this comes from researchers at MIT[4]. They have discovered that all our habits are driven by the same simple neurological loop. This "habit loop" consists of three components:

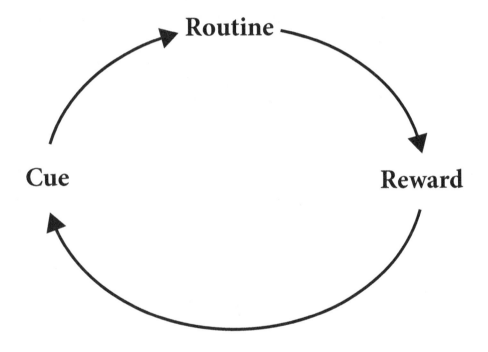

1. A cue, which is the trigger that starts your habit
2. A routine, which is the habit itself
3. A reward, which is the benefit you gain from doing the habit

If you perceive the reward as positive, you'll want to repeat the loop again the next time the same cue shows up. When this sequence gets repeated enough times, it will become automatic and a habit will be formed.

Phone application developers are very aware of this and design their apps in a way that plays right into our psychology to get us hooked on their product.

If you tend to respond immediately to notifications on your phone, you know what I'm talking about. It doesn't matter much what you've got going on at that moment; the urge you get from the notification is enough to make you abort what you're doing and check your phone instead.

Here's how the habit loop works in this scenario: your phone gives off a notification sound (cue), you pick up your phone and check the notification (routine), and get to know what the notification is about (reward).

Knowing that all your habits work this way is very powerful, because it allows you to experiment deliberately with different cues, routines, and rewards until you get them to work for you.

In the next couple of pages, you'll get to learn the best strategies scientists have found for doing just that.

Step 1: Pick Your Habit

You probably have an idea of the change you want to create in your life. Otherwise, you wouldn't be reading this book. But before definitely deciding what habit to start working on first, I want to share an idea that will greatly enhance the chances for you to get some really explosive results from this book.

Have you ever noticed how some habits tend to "spill over" and create positive effects across all areas of your life? In his book, *The Power of Habit*, author and habit expert Charles Duhigg refers to these behaviors as "keystone habits."[5]

For me, exercise is a huge keystone habit. I know this because whenever I work out regularly, all the other aspects of my life seem to fall naturally into place by themselves: I sleep better, I eat better, I'm way more productive, and I enjoy life more in general.

So, to get a flying start on your habit change, I highly recommend you begin with a keystone habit. Ask yourself what habit seemed to have had this positive ripple effect in your life in the past. It could be exercise, but it could also be practicing meditation, getting proper sleep, decluttering your environment, adjusting your eating and drinking habits, or something else entirely.

If you can think of several keystone habits, that's great, but I encourage you to start working on just one of them the first time you read this book. There's nothing wrong with going after several habits at once, but going through the process with just one habit is very helpful because it keeps things simple and reduces the risk of your becoming overwhelmed.

When you've successfully established one habit, you can then start experimenting with adding several others.

Step 1: Pick Your Habit

1. Reflect on your keystone habits. What behaviors have "spilled over" and created a ripple effect of positive change in all areas of your life in the past?

2. Pick just one habit. This is the habit you will be working on while reading this book for the first time.

Step 2: Start Ridiculously Small

A parole board judge is just about to make a final decision on whether or not to approve a criminal for parole. What do you think will affect this decision the most?

Maybe the crime committed? Or the particular law that was broken? Perhaps the criminal's recent behavior in prison?

These are all reasonable guesses, but as it turns out, they are not even close. No, the most important factor that will decide the outcome for the criminal is instead something as seemingly trivial as the time of day.

More precisely, the chances of getting a favorable ruling will be about 65 percent in the morning and right after lunch. Should the case come up just before lunch or late in the day, the criminal's chances will instead be close to zero.

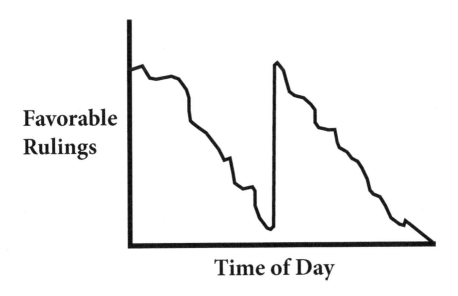

Favorable Rulings

Time of Day

And this isn't true just for some rare, isolated events. The researchers who noticed this trend found that it held true for more than eleven hundred cases, no matter what the crime was.[6] How could this be?

Research has shown that willpower works like a muscle. This idea is known as ego-depletion[7] and explains that just like a physical muscle, your willpower gets increasingly tired the more you put it to use.

You can think of your willpower as a cell phone battery that gets charged when you rest. When you wake up in the morning, your willpower battery will usually be full. As you get out of bed and start your day, your battery level will drop a bit for every decision that you make throughout your day.

And this was what was happening to the parole board judges. As they progressed through their day, making hard decisions about which criminals should get parole and which criminals shouldn't, their willpower became more and more depleted.

The less willpower energy they happened to have at the moment, the less inclined they were to give a favorable ruling. After all, it makes sense to play it safe and keep everyone locked up if you're too tired to make a good decision.

What we can learn from this is that willpower isn't some trait that you either have or don't have. Rather, it's something that fluctuates throughout your day.

So, to ensure that you have sufficient willpower for your habit, it's a good idea to do it at a time when you know that your willpower is high. However, since you can't know for sure that you're always well rested and full of energy, an even better approach is to avoid relying on willpower at all. How?

By starting so ridiculously small that when it's time to do it, it would be silly to say no.[8] This strategy is very powerful because it ensures that your habit won't fail because of random fluctuations in your willpower.

Another benefit of starting really small is it gets you over that initial hurdle of just getting started. You've probably often experienced firsthand that getting started doing something is the hard part. Once you're up and running, it doesn't require much effort at all. For example, getting to the gym can be tough, but once you're there, the actual workout itself usually isn't that bad.

Another benefit you'll notice when using this strategy is that many times, you'll end up doing a lot more than you had initially planned to. For example, if your habit is to read one page in a book, you're likely to end up reading several pages or even the entire chapter. This is because starting small also takes advantage of what psychologists call the Zeigarnik effect, which is our natural tendency to want to finish what we've started and not yet completed.[9]

Step 2: Start Ridiculously Small

Make your habit so tiny that you can easily complete it every day without having to rely on willpower. When I say small, I mean really small. Floss one tooth, do one minute of meditation, take a two-minute walk—you get the idea.

Then, if you feel like doing more once you've completed your small habit on a given day, by all means go ahead and do it. This is the beauty of the Zeigarnik effect.

But whatever you do, do not increase the difficulty of your habit when you're just getting started. No matter what you want this habit to look like down the line, focus on establishing the actual behavior first. If you just stick to the process, your small habit will naturally expand into the bigger behavior with time.

Step 3: Build a Chain

When a young comic asked Jerry Seinfeld for advice on how to be a better comic, Seinfeld answered that the way to be a better comic is to create better jokes and the way to create better jokes is to write every day. The young comic recounts Seinfeld's explanation of his system:

> He told me to get a big wall calendar that has a whole year on one page and hang it on a prominent wall. The next step was to get a big red magic marker.

> He said for each day that I do my task of writing, I get to put a big red X over that day. "After a few days you'll have a chain. Just keep at it and the chain will grow longer every day. You'll like seeing that chain, especially when you get a few weeks under your belt. Your only job next is to not break the chain."[10]

This simple strategy is quite brilliant because it plays right into a very interesting aspect of human psychology known in behavioral economics as the sunk cost fallacy. This fallacy can be defined as "the tendency to make decisions about the current situation based on what was previously invested in it."[11]

Here are a few examples to illustrate how this fallacy makes for irrational decisions:

- "I'm full, but I might as well keep eating because I've paid for the food."

- "This movie is terrible, but I might as well watch the whole thing because I've watched an hour of it already."

- "The class is useless, but since I've already paid for it I might as well keep going."

- "I'm going to stay in this bad relationship because I've already invested so much in the other person."

Clearly, the sunk cost fallacy can be a big problem, but we can also get it to work in our favor. And this is precisely where Seinfeld's strategy shines. Every time you put that "big red X" on your calendar, you've invested yet another day into your chain. The longer your chain gets, the harder it will be for you to skip a day as you don't want to lose your investment.

Step 3: Build a Chain

Create a chain-building system. There are two ways you can do this:

1. Get a physical wall calendar. Hang it on a wall where you will see it often and put a pen right next to it so you can easily track your progress every day.

2. Download a habit tracker. If you prefer working digitally, you can download an app that measures your progress. There are plenty of habit-tracking apps out there, but my favorite is Coach.me.

Once you've done this, it's important that each time you complete your habit, you immediately add a new X to your chain. If you stick to this, it likely won't be long before you find yourself pushing through even on uninspired days, just to keep your chain going.

Step 4: Choose a Trigger

Now we get to the first part of the habit loop, which is the trigger that will remind you to initiate the behavior. One of the biggest mistakes people make when they're trying to create a new habit is that they set a very vague intention. Telling yourself, "I should probably work out tomorrow after work" will never create and solidify a big change in your life.

To create a new habit and make it stick, you need to decide on a very specific cue that reminds you to do it, over and over again. The reason creating a very specific trigger for your habit is so useful is that it takes out all the mental effort. Instead of having to think about when, where, why, and if you're going to do the habit on a given day, you just follow a predetermined course of action and get it done without wasting your limited mental energy.

Following are three very effective, science-backed ways to create powerful cues.

1. Implementation Intentions

Professor of psychology Peter Gollwitzer focuses his research on how goals and plans affect cognition, emotion, and behavior. He has found that people who write down exactly when and where they intend to do a certain habit are much more likely to follow through.[12]

This powerful strategy is also deceptively simple. All you do is reframe your goals as "if-then" statements. The "if" represents a situational cue and the "then" is your planned response to that cue. Here are some examples:

- "Journal daily" becomes, "If I'm in bed at night, then I'll write in my journal."
- "Be more patient" becomes, "If I start feeling stressed, then I'll focus on taking three deep breaths."

- "Read more" becomes, "If I sit down on the living room couch, then I'll pick up an awesome book."

To use implementation intention as your cue, you can use either an internal cue (such as a strong feeling) or an external cue (such a particular time, place, object, or person).

2. Habit Stacking

This strategy is similar to implementation intentions, but here you "stack" your new behavior to an already established habit [13]. We're looking to fill in this sentence:

After/Before [established habit], I will [new habit].

For example, you could implement stacking into your daily routines:

- "Before I take my morning shower, I will do five pushups."
- "Before I brush my teeth, I will floss my teeth."
- "After I set my alarm clock, I will meditate for one minute."
- "After I get into bed, I will read two pages in a book."

To use habit stacking write down a list of habits that you do every day without fail. Then go through that list and find the most suitable one to stack your new habit together with.

3. Scheduling

This last technique for creating a habit cue may seem very obvious, yet very few people put it to use. Here's the thing: If you want to make sure something gets done, you put it on your calendar, right? Well, the same goes for a new habit. If your new behavior is truly important to you, it deserves a spot among the other important things in your calendar. Why? There are several reasons:

- It shows that you are serious about this change and that it has just the same priority in your life as, for example, important business meetings. It's a way to tell yourself that you're done dabbling with vague intentions and that you're serious about making this happen.

- We're all susceptible to the "planning fallacy,"[14] a mental bias that makes us underestimate how much time things actually take. When you pre-commit to your habit this way, it forces you to take stock of how much time you actually have for your new habit and reduces the risk overly optimistic planning.

- It eliminates future decisions. Making decisions, even trivial ones, decreases our mental energy.[15] When you commit to a schedule, you free up a lot of mental energy that can be used for more important decisions than whether to do your habit.

To use scheduling as your trigger, get out your calendar and specify exactly when and where your habit will be taking place. If you don't have one, I recommend using Google Calendar and setting a notification for your new habit to make sure you don't miss it.

Step 4: Choose a Trigger

Choose a trigger for your habit using an implementation intention, habit stacking, or scheduling. Which one you choose depends on what habit you're trying to create and what works best for you personally. It's time to put on your white coat and start experimenting. Make your best guess as to which trigger should work best for you and your habit and then start trying it out in the real world. If it works, great! If it doesn't, you can always change it later.

Step 5: Create a Reward

Now that you've decided on a trigger and the tiny habit that will follow it, it's time to get to work on the last part of the habit loop, which is the reward.

In behavioral theory, reinforcement is "the act of following a response with a reinforcer."[16] This is one of the primary tools in what psychologists refer to as operant conditioning,[17] and it's also what we will be using to automate the habit you're working on so you'll stick to it consistently.

In particular, what we'll be using to do this is our feelings. Now, we all know that our feelings tend to affect the way we act. But did you know that the opposite is also true? Researchers have found that the body language we use, our facial expressions, and even our tone of voice affect our emotions in a big way. Some fascinating studies have shown that:

- By using powerful posture, you increase the dominance hormone testosterone while at the same time decreasing the stress hormone cortisol;[18]

- When you frown for a long time, you're more likely to experience aggressive feelings;[19] and

- Speaking at a lower pitch makes you feel more powerful.[20]

These findings are important, because we can use them to our advantage when establishing new habits. How? By celebrating in a way that stirs up positive emotions immediately after every successful attempt to perform it. When you do this, you get your brain to associate the accomplishment of your habit with feeling good. Your habit becomes reinforced, and you'll be more likely to do it again in the future.

How exactly to celebrate is highly individual and a skill you'll need to practice and experiment with to get good at. (You'll find a list of suggestions at the end of this chapter.) What's important is that you find a way to celebrate that feels authentic to you. If it seems silly, you won't create the positive emotions you need to make the celebration effective.

A lot of people have problems with this step, because they feel like doing such a tiny habit is no real cause for celebration. Stanford University psychologist and behavior expert BJ Fogg suggests you think of it this way:

> The fact that you're learning to change your behavior is a big deal. Think how rare a skill it is. Think how long behavior change has eluded you. And now you are succeeding.

So don't celebrate that one tooth is cleaner. Instead, celebrate that you have taken another step forward to improve your life.[21]

Step 5: Create a Reward

Create your reward. Then use it to celebrate immediately after each successful attempt of completing your habit. You know how often athletes celebrate and how they do it immediately after they've made a great effort? That's what we're looking for here!

Here are some of Fogg's suggestions:

- Do a physical movement signifying victory (pump your fist, clap your hands, or give yourself a thumbs up).
- Yell something out loud ('Awesome job!', 'I rock!' 'Go, me!').
- Vocalize your own fanfare ('Do do do dooo!').
- Imagine a roaring crowd rooting for you.
- Mirror the facial expression of a happy person (smile or laugh). [22]

Of course, these are just suggestions. If you want, you can combine several of them or do something else entirely. If it doesn't feel right to you, keep trying new ways to celebrate until you've found a way that works for you.

Step 6: Set Up a Token Economy

In his book, The Now Habit, psychologist Neil Fiore writes about how he and his fellow psychology students used to agonize for days over papers that would eventually take less than two hours to write.

It didn't matter how bright they were or how many theories of human behavior they learned. When it came to their own thoughts, feelings, and behavior, they always struggled.

When looking for a solution to this problem, Fiore learned that B. F. Skinner, the founder of modern behaviorism, used a time clock connected to his chair to "punch in" each time he sat down to work.

Whenever he left the chair, the clock would stop, as if here were "punching out". This allowed Skinner to measure his time much like how lawyers and architects do when keeping track of the time to charge their clients.

Skinner then recorded his times in flow charts and awarded himself with a gold star each time he completed a small segment of work.[23]

This strategy of giving out gold stars (or any symbol you see fit) for rewarding and reinforcing good behavior is known in psychology as a token economy.[24] The tokens themselves have no intrinsic value, but can later be exchanged for "backup reinforcers" in the form of actual rewards.

As I've mentioned before, rewarding yourself for good behavior is a crucial part of making it stick, and if we're going to do it, why not use the method the founder of modern behaviorism used for his own work?

Step 6: Set Up a Token Economy

1. Create specific and measurable minimum daily quotas. Before you can reward a step in the right direction, you'll have to determine what that step is exactly and how you're going to measure it. One way to do this that is similar to B. F. Skinner's approach is to use

the Pomodoro Technique and give yourself a set number of tokens for each completed twenty-five-minute session.[25]

2. Get some kind of token to reward yourself with. This could be gold stars, coins, poker chips, or something else you happen to have laying around the house. Each time you successfully reach your minimum daily quota, reward yourself with a certain number of tokens. Then start stacking your tokens where you can see them every day to create an inspiring visual representation of your progress that you'll want to keep building every day.

3. Set up your backup reinforcers. These are the rewards you get to exchange your tokens for. The key here is to reward yourself with things that keep you moving toward, and not away from, your long-term goal. In other words, don't celebrate a good week of running by eating chocolate cake but rather by getting a new piece of running equipment. Create a list of backup reinforcers that allows you to progressively build the identity of the person you want to become. For the running example, new equipment and opportunities could be "redeemed" with a certain number of tokens:

    - Water bottle = 5 tokens
    - Running socks = 10 tokens
    - Portable music player = 15 tokens
    - Pedometer = 20 tokens
    - Running shoes = 100 tokens
    - Entry to marathon = 500 tokens

This is not a perfect token economy by any means, but I'm sure you get the point. What's important is that you create a list of rewards that give you an increasing sense of accomplishment and competence.

Step 7: Schedule a Weekly Review

How long does it take to form a new habit? When it comes to this question, there is a lot of false information out there. One popular estimate that tends to keep coming up is twenty-one days. Another number that's been showing up a lot lately is sixty-six days.

But the truth is, practical as it would be, you simply can't assign a given number of days and expect it to be accurate every time, regardless of who you are, where you are, and what habit you're trying to create. There are just too many variables affecting the outcome for this to be possible.

The "sixty-six days to form a habit" hype mentioned above comes from a 2009 study conducted by researchers at the University College of London.[26] But the specific number of sixty-six days is, unfortunately, a gross oversimplification of the results of the study. What the researchers did find was that it took the participants on average sixty-six days to automate their desired behavior, but for any given person or habit it can take anywhere from 18 to 254 days.

So, if you want to set your expectations right, you should know that it might well take you upward of eight months to build a new behavior that becomes fully automatic. But here's the thing: there's no need to get disheartened by this. Why? Because habits are a process, not an event. This is not something you set out to do for some specific number of days and then forget about. Lasting change never works that way.

Sometimes the habit will feel completely effortless. At other times, it'll be hard work. When you accept this fact and start embracing a longer timeline for your habit, you won't get as bogged down when you run into the setbacks and obstacles that will inevitably show up from time to time.

Instead of worrying about some arbitrary number of days, you're way better off if you create a system that works and then fall in love with the process of consistently executing on that system. In other words, the key to establishing your new habit is to stop obsessing over the results you want and instead start obsessing over showing up every day.

That's the paradox: the moment you stop worrying about the results you want tends to be the moment you can start to make progress toward them. A very effective way to make this shift is to self-monitor your progress,[27] and that's what we'll be focusing on in this step.

Step 7: Schedule a Weekly Review

Schedule ten to fifteen minutes every week to examine the progress you're making on your habit. Ideally, this would be the same time every week. Your weekly review will consist of two simple steps:

1. Celebrate your wins, big or small, and exchange your tokens for rewards.

2. Reflect on the days you missed and adjust your habit so you'll be likelier to succeed next week.

You will learn more about how to adjust your habit in the next couple of pages. But before you keep on reading, get out your calendar and schedule in your weekly review. Make sure you plan it the same way you would with anything important. Because this *is* important, right?

Step 8: Design Your Environment

During the Vietnam War, more than 15 percent of U.S. soldiers developed a heroin addiction. This discovery shocked the American public and President Richard Nixon announced the creation of a new office called the Special Action Office of Drug Abuse Prevention. This office was created to work for prevention and rehabilitation of drug addictions as well as researching and tracking the paths of the addicted soldiers when they returned home. It was this last part, the tracking of returning troops, which led to some fascinating, and surprising, insights.

What the researchers found was that when the soldiers returned home, 95 percent of them kicked their addiction almost overnight![28] This finding was very unexpected as it completely contradicted the usual patterns of addictions at the time. A typical heroin addict would enter a clinic and get clean, but as soon as they returned home, the risk of falling back into addiction was 90 percent or higher. So, the pattern the Vietnam soldiers were displaying were almost the exact opposite. What was the cause of these strange results? In short, their environment.

In Vietnam, the soldiers spent their days in an environment that drove them toward heroin use. They were put under extreme stress, became friends with other soldiers who were heroin users, and the drug was also readily available. Using heroin became their new normal. When the soldiers later returned home, suddenly they found themselves in an entirely different environment. In these surroundings, there weren't any triggers promoting heroin use, and this helped the soldiers drop their addiction.

If you compare this scenario with the situation of a typical drug user, it makes sense that they tend to relapse. The clinic does a good job of removing harmful triggers and makes it easier to get clean, but as soon as this person returns home, all their old triggers will reappear in their environment and make relapse so much more likely. The lesson here is that our surroundings heavily influence our behavior, often without us being consciously aware of it. The triggers in our environment are constantly nudging us one way or another, and we can use this to our advantage.

In his book *Finding Flow*, professor of psychology Mihaly Csikszentmihalyi writes about what he calls the "activation energy" of habits. The idea is that the bigger the obstacles standing in the way of your desired behavior, the more activation energy you will need to muster up and the less likely you'll be to do it. He explains that "if a person is too tired, anxious, or lacks the discipline to overcome that initial obstacle, he or she will have to settle for something that, although less enjoyable, is more accessible."[29]

So, to make sure your habit gets done, you need to lower the activation energy required to do it. In plain English, this means changing your environment so that your habit becomes easier to do. The more you can lower (or even eliminate) the activation energy needed for your habit, the likelier you'll be to get it done.

Step 8: Design Your Environment

Manipulate your environment in at least one way that decreases the activation energy of your habit. Once you start experimenting with this, you'll probably find that even tiny changes in your surroundings can make a huge difference in your behavior. Here are a few examples of changes to make:

- If you want to read two pages, place the book right where you usually sit.
- If you want to exercise for five minutes in the morning, put your workout clothes next to your bed.
- If you want to meditate for two minutes in the morning, put your meditation cushion in place the night before.
- If you want to eat less, get smaller plates.
- If you want to sleep better, make your bedroom slightly cool and pitch black.

Step 9: Make Procrastination Difficult

Another study that brilliantly illustrates the power of environment on our behavior was conducted at a hospital in Boston. In this study, researchers secretly manipulated the environment of the hospital cafeteria over a period of six months. While doing this, they ended up helping thousands of people develop healthier eating and drinking habits. How?

At the beginning of the study, the three main refrigerators in the cafeteria were filled with soda. The researchers added water to these fridges and also placed baskets with bottled water throughout the room. The result of these small tweaks in the environment was that in the following three months, soda sales dropped by 11 percent while bottled water sales went up by 26 percent. The researchers also made adjustments in the food options and saw similar results.[30]

Nobody told the cafeteria visitors what to do. The researchers just changed the environment to promote healthier options and the customers adjusted their behaviors accordingly. If your environment supports a healthy behavior, then that's usually what you'll end up doing.

Unfortunately, this is also true for behaviors that we don't want. When we procrastinate, it's very often also just the result of us responding to our environment. If there are snacks on the living room table, we're likely to eat them. If we get an e-mail notification, we're likely to click it. If our phone rings in the middle of creative work, we're likely to drop what we're doing and answer it.

In the last step, you learned how to lower the activation energy of your habit. In this step, your task is to raise the activation energy of competing behaviors. What you're looking to do is make competing, unwanted behaviors harder to do and, as a result, less likely. Take a moment to think about all the behaviors you could end up turning to instead of your habit and then increase the activation energy of these to the point where you won't want to do them.

Step 9: Make Procrastination Difficult

Change your environment in at least one way that makes your unwanted behaviors harder to do. Following are some examples:

- If snoozing is causing you to miss your morning exercise, put the alarm clock in the next room.

- If social media is interrupting your meditation practice, turn off the notifications on your phone.

- If TV is stopping you from reading your book, put the remote control in another room (or put the TV in the garage).

Put the TV in the garage? Yup, I said it. How much you turn up the activation energy of your undesired behaviors is, of course, up to you. But if your new habit is truly important to you, don't be afraid to take some drastic actions regarding your environment to support it.

Step 10: Surround Yourself with Role Models

Have you ever noticed how people who spend a lot of time together tend to become more and more alike? Not just in their appearance but in their thoughts, values, and goals. Jim Rohn used to say, "You are the average of the five people you spend the most time with," and contemporary science has shown that there is a lot of truth to this statement.

In a study conducted by psychologist James Shah, college students were interviewed to determine how much their fathers valued high achievement. Shah found that when the students were unconsciously exposed to their fathers' names right before performing a number of difficult tasks, those students who associated their dads with high achievement worked harder and performed better than the other students. This effect was stronger the closer the students reported being to their dads.

Interestingly, when the tasks were completed, they had no idea that they had been working particularly hard. Instead, the inclination to do well was triggered only by unconscious thoughts about their fathers and executed entirely without awareness of this.[31]

And it turns out this works the other way around, too. Unconsciously thinking about someone close to you who does *not* approve of a particular behavior can inhibit you from pursuing it. If your unconscious mind is envisioning your disappointed mother, you'll be less likely to leave dishes in the sink.

Even the goals of people you don't know can have a big impact on what goals you decide to pursue. Psychologists refer to this as goal contagion: our tendency to be more likely to pursue a goal just by seeing someone else doing it.

In one of the first studies of goal contagion, a group of Dutch participants were asked to read a short story about Johan, a college student who was about to go on a vacation with his friends. This story came in two versions.

In the first version, Johan was going to a farm in his village to work for a month before going on the trip. This information implied that Johan had the goal of earning some money to be able to go on his trip. In the second version, Johan was instead going to spend that same month at a community center doing volunteer work.

After reading one of the two stories, the participants got the opportunity to earn some money by completing a computer task as quickly as possible. Those who had read the story where Johan had the goal of making money were 10 percent faster than those who had read the story in which Johan was a volunteer. Without realizing it on a conscious level, the faster participants had been influenced by Johan's contagious goal to make money and had gone after it themselves.[32]

The effect other people's goals have on you can be quite extraordinary. One study found that if you have a friend who becomes obese, your risk of also becoming obese increases by 57 percent—even if your friend lives hundreds of miles away![33]

Without realizing it, we are constantly conforming to the people around us and taking on their goals. That's why it's crucial to surround yourself with positive influences. If you want to create healthy habits but all of your friends are unhealthy, you'll be at a huge disadvantage. If you have big goals you want to achieve in your life but most of the people around you are slackers, you'll always be fighting an uphill battle.

The people you surround yourself with determine what's normal for you. So if you want to get remarkable results, you need remarkable people around you.

Here's probably the most powerful strategy in this entire book: fill your environment with people who are already at the level you want to be (or, at least, are passionately pursuing the same goals as you are) and watch how it transforms everything about you. Before you know it, you'll adapt to the new people around you and unconsciously raise your standards to match what's normal in this new environment. Once you do, it's only a matter of time before you establish any habit you want.

Step 10: Surround Yourself With Role Models

Write down the names of one to five people you know you should be spending more time with. If you can't think of anyone, list out the places, events, or online communities where you could connect with these people. Then take the first step by immediately reaching out to at least one person.

Step 11: Turn Accomplices into Supporters

You know how certain people have the ability to light up a room just by walking through the door? And how some other people have the exact opposite effect? Isn't it fascinating how these people can have such a huge impact on the atmosphere in the room just by being present?

Research has shown that this is because of a natural tendency we have to converge emotionally with each other.[34] This tendency is referred to as emotional contagion and happens in an automatic process where we mimic and synchronize the expressions, vocalizations, postures, and movements of the people around us. This, in turn, leads us to "tune in" to the emotions of everyone else.

You might be having a splendid day and feel on top of the world, but if you walk into an environment where everyone else is feeling down, you will inevitably pick up on this and start feeling worse yourself. At the end of the day, your day might well have turned for the worse.

Now think about the implications of this. How does this emotional contagion affect your general quality of life if you spend most (or all of) your time in the presence of negative people? How do you think it affects how you feel and perform every day?

What would it mean to you if you instead were always surrounded with excited, positive, and encouraging people? How would that impact your well-being? What would it mean to always have people to count on for support and encouragement? Just imagine how much this second scenario would do for your performance and overall happiness.

Still, most of us never proactively shape our social surroundings. And that's a shame, because just like the goals of other people affect our behaviors, so do the emotions and attitudes they bring to the relationship.

In the previous chapter, you took the first step to surround yourself with new, positive influences to support your new habit. This step is about changing your already existing social connections. If you have a lot of encouraging people around you, that's great, and we'll get more in-depth about how you can use this more effectively to your advantage in the next couple of pages. But if you happen to have a lot of negative influences around you, now is the time to do something about it by doing either of the following:

1. Turn them into supporters. Explain the role the person is playing in making your change harder for you and then share how you'd like them to help you succeed. A lot of times, a friendly conversation is all that's needed to gain a new supporter.

2. Distance yourself. If someone for some reason can't or won't support your efforts, you need to separate yourself from them. Often, this occurs naturally as you make changes in your life but at times you're going to have to deliberately distance yourself from people who are actively keeping you from creating the change you want.

Step 11: Turn Accomplices into Supporters

Write down a list of one to five people that currently aren't as supportive as you'd like. Then take the first step immediately by reaching out to the first person on your list and ask them to support you in the way you need. If someone isn't willing or able to support you, limit the time you spend with that person as much as you can.

Step 12: Create a Commitment Contract

In a study conducted in the Philippines, researchers had surveyors approach people on the streets with an offer of opening a bank account that paid zero interest. The people who chose to open this type of bank account committed to losing all the money they had deposited if their urine showed any evidence of smoking six months later. So, to recap the offer, that's a bank account with no interest, a good chance of losing your money, plus the discomfort of having to go through a urine test.

Not a very appealing offer, right? Still, more than 10 percent of people approached agreed to sign up for an account. Not a bad turnout for such a poor deal. Even more surprising, though, were the results of the experiment: right around 30 percent of the participants ended up quitting their smoking habit because of it.[35] For this kind of behavior change, that's a huge success rate—higher than is the case with more traditional smoking-cessation aids like nicotine patches.

And when you think about it, it makes sense that this kind of "commitment contract" would be a great motivator to change behavior. To illustrate this, let's have a look at two scenarios:

1. It's 6:00 a.m. on a random Monday morning, and you get brutally interrupted from your deep sleep. While you're fumbling to turn off the alarm, you remember last night's promise to yourself to hit the gym before work.

2. It's 6:00 a.m. on a random Monday morning, and you get brutally interrupted from your deep sleep. While you're fumbling to turn off the alarm, you remember that you have a plane to catch for an important business meeting.

If you're like most people, you'll be much more likely to get out of bed in scenario number two. This is because this situation comes with much greater immediate consequences. We usually don't perceive letting ourselves off the hook for going to the gym as a big deal. We've done it many times before, and the only ones suffering from doing so will be us.

But in the second scenario, the immediate consequences are much greater. Not only does it have a very tangible deadline (the time the gate closes) but you're also financially and emotionally invested. If you don't show up, you'll have to deal with possible financial setbacks and the public embarrassment of letting people down and not sticking to your word.

In the first scenario, it's easy to start rationalizing with yourself about why you need the extra sleep and that it's probably a better idea to exercise after work instead (even though in reality, you very rarely manage to make it to the gym after a long day at work). In the second scenario, all those considerations are off the table. The immediate consequences of staying in bed are simply too high.

This is why using a commitment contract like the researchers offered in the study I mentioned earlier is such a powerful tool for behavior change: it enables you to create self-imposed, immediate consequences for procrastinating.

Let's imagine the first scenario again. Only this time, you remember that you've already committed to following through by promising a friend to meet up at the gym at 7:00 a.m. Or by sending $50 to another friend each time you fail to stick to your workout routine. Or by committing publicly to your family/blog readers/Facebook friends that you will be sticking to your exercise routine for at least thirty days. Or, if necessary, a combination of all of the above. Suddenly, going back to sleep won't seem as appealing anymore.

Step 12: Create a Commitment Contract

Your contract should consist of three parts:

1. Your goal: the habit you want to create. This is where you commit to the tiny daily steps you've decided on earlier in this book.

2. Something at stake: this could be cold, hard cash or your reputation (or a combination of both).

3. A referee: the person who will hold you accountable to your goal. Choose someone who you know will be strict but fair.

Here's an outline you can use:

Commitment Contract

I commit to _____. (For example, "Performing one minute of meditation every day for a month.")

If I don't do this, I will _____. (For example, "Send a friend $50 dollars and/or let my social network know that I failed.")

My referee will be _____. (For example, "A friend who won't have any problems holding me accountable.")

Next, print this contract out and put it somewhere you will see it every day. If you'd prefer a digital alternative, you can use StickK.com. This service lets you create a commitment contract online, and, if you want to raise the stakes even more, donate money to a charity you don't like if you fail. How's that for a clever way to increase the immediate consequences of failing?

Step 13: Get Accountability

Back in the 1950s, researcher Henry Landsberger did a study and analysis of data from experiments conducted between 1924 and 1932 at the Hawthorne Works near Chicago by industrial researcher and psychologist Elton Mayo.

The purpose of these tests had initially been to determine whether more light in the building positively affected the productivity of the workers. Mayo did find that the workers increased their output when they were exposed to more light. Interestingly though, they also increased their production when they were exposed to *less* light. What was going on?

As it turned out, it didn't matter what changes the researchers made. The lighting levels or any other variable they would experiment with was irrelevant. As long as they did something, the productivity of the workers would spike.[36]

This tendency would later be named the Hawthorne effect, and the work of Mayo and Landsberger would become foundational in a field in social science known as industrial psychology. What the Hawthorne effect teaches us is that we perform better by the mere fact that we are aware that we are under observation by others.

This is why accountability is such a powerful force when it comes to creating change and establishing new habits. When someone else is tracking your progress and making sure you stick to what you set out to do, you'll be much more likely to follow through.

Step 13: Get Accountability

In the previous step, you created a commitment contract. Now is the time to get it into the hands of at least one other person to hold you accountable. Here are some ideas for how to do this:

- Print it out and give it to your friends.
- Find an accountability partner or group and share it with them.
- Join an online community related to your habit and post it in the forums.
- Send it to a mentor.
- Get a coach and ask for accountability.
- Post it on social media.
- Start a blog and give the URL to a group of supporters.

Don't go it alone. Make sure you have at least one person who is continually following up on your progress and making sure you're sticking to your plan.

Step 14: Prevent Mental Loopholes

Have you ever noticed how easy it is to fall for the "tomorrow loophole?"

How many times have you told yourself things like:

- "I'm too tired to work out today, and I could always do it tomorrow";
- "I really should stick to my diet, but those cupcakes look awfully delicious. I'll make sure to make up for it tomorrow"; and
- "This project is going to need a lot of work, but I'm sure I can get up earlier and start it tomorrow."

For some reason, we have this highly irrational overconfidence that the things we won't get done right here and now will somehow be easier tomorrow, next week, or even next year.

One study illustrated this tendency perfectly. When the subjects were asked to make a shopping list for what they were going to eat next week, they were inclined to choose a healthy snack over an unhealthy one. Of course, when they were asked what they would choose right now, they were much more likely to choose the unhealthy snack.[37] We want to make the right choice—as long as we don't have to make it right now.

And the tomorrow loophole is just one of the excuses we employ to get off the hook from doing our habit at a given moment. In her book, *Better Than Before*, author Gretchen Rubin lists the most popular loopholes:

- Moral licensing. You give yourself permission to do something "bad" because you've done something "good." For example, "I've been so good at sticking to my diet that I deserve to eat these potato chips."
- False choice. You pose two activities in opposition as if you have to make an either-or decision, even though the two aren't necessarily

in conflict. For example, "I've been so busy at work, I haven't been exercising."

- Lack of control. You tell yourself that your lack of control over the situation and circumstances forces you to break your habit. For example, "I'd go for a run right now if I could, but it's raining outside."

- Arranging to fail. Instead of avoiding a temptation, you plan in a way that you succumb. For example, "I'll watch a Youtube video for 10 minutes before I start studying."

- "This doesn't count." You tell yourself that for some reason, this particular circumstance doesn't count. For example, "I'm on vacation, so I'll put off the meditation until I get back."

- Questionable assumption. You make an assumption that negatively influences your habit. For example, "I have to go to work in one hour, and I can't get anything worthwhile done before then."

- Concern for others. You tell yourself that you're acting out of consideration for others. For example, "It would be rude not to drink at my friend's party."

- Fake self-actualization. You accept a failure of your habit by disguising it as an embrace of life. For example, "Why shouldn't I treat myself with this? You only live once!"

- "One-coin." You devalue the meaning of one single attempt. For example, "I can skip the gym today, one workout won't matter."[38]

Step 14: Prevent Mental Loopholes

Reading about these mental loopholes is usually a significant first step because it makes you much more aware of this tendency in yourself. Now, it's all about becoming very skeptical about your brain's rationalizations the moment they show up.

Always remember that you are not your thoughts and that your thoughts are not necessarily right or even looking out for your best long-term interests. Get into the habit of asking, "Is this thought true, or is my brain simply seeking the path of least resistance?"

Create specific if-then "mini actions" to protect your habit from mental loopholes. For example:

- If my brain tries talk to me into staying in bed when the alarm goes off, then I will get up and stay up for ten minutes before deciding whether or not to sleep in.

- If my brain tries to convince me to skip my daily run, then I will put on my shoes and go outside before deciding.

- If my brain tells me I deserve a glass of wine after a stressful day, then I will meditate for ten minutes first.

Pre-committing in this way can be very helpful because it gives cravings some extra time to pass while directing you to healthier and more productive behaviors by default. It can also help you to just get started on the habit, which is usually the hardest part.

Step 15: Plan for Failure

Now, no matter how well you've prepared yourself in the previous steps, it's crucial to realize that there's a good chance you'll still find yourself messing up and breaking your hard-earned chain from time to time. When this happens, you'll likely be very vulnerable to what psychologists have given the catchy name the what-the-hell effect.

One clever study did an excellent job of illustrating how this effect works. The researchers did an experiment in which they asked their participants not to eat beforehand and then treated them all to the same exact size slice of pizza. Some of the participants were dieters and some were not.

After finishing their pizza, participants were all asked to taste and rate some cookies. But the researchers didn't care about how the cookies were rated. Instead, they measured how many of the cookies each participant ended up eating.

That's because the researchers had carried out a little trick: even though all of the participants had been given the same slice of pizza, some of them had been made to believe it looked larger by comparison. This made some of the participants think they had eaten more than they had, even though in reality they had all eaten the same amount.

When the cookies were rated later on, it turned out that the participants who were on a diet and believed they had blown their limit ended up eating more cookies than the people who weren't on a diet. In fact, they ate over 50 percent more! On the other hand, the dieters who thought they were still safely within their limit ate about the same number of cookies as the non-dieters.[39]

I bet there's a good chance you can relate to this tendency when you think back on your attempts to create new habits in your life. In the beginning, it feels great, and you get some nice momentum going. But then, as soon as you miss a day, you're suddenly way more likely to give up on all your efforts entirely.

This is, of course, highly irrational. Just because you miss one attempt doesn't mean all of your previous efforts doesn't count and that you should let them go to waste. Research has shown that missing one single opportunity to perform a behavior doesn't affect the habit formation process in and of itself.[40] This only becomes an obstacle when you let it.

And herein lies the greatest paradox of habit creation. Because, as you may remember from the previous step, one of the mental loopholes, one-coin, means you devalue the importance of a single attempt. And as it turns out, this is absolutely true. If you miss the gym one time, it won't matter much at all. And yet, it will, because it puts you in danger of the what-the-hell effect.

The way to deal with this is to get a bit contradictory in your approach. Defend your chain as if it's super important (because it is), but if you mess up one time, realize that isn't a big deal (because it isn't). Do everything in your power to build as long a chain as possible, but if you find yourself in the situation where you've broken it, simply start a new one right away.

There's no point in ruminating over a missed attempt because stacking guilt and shame on top of what you perceive as a poor performance only makes it harder to get back on track.[41] Let the past be in the past, forgive yourself quickly and get back in the game as fast as you can.

Step 15: Plan for Failure

Decide right now that when you've missed an attempt of completing your daily tiny habit, you will focus on the total number of days you've successfully completed rather than the fact that you've broken your chain. Celebrate what went well, forgive yourself for what didn't, and then get right back into the action.

Grab Your Free Workbook

And so, we've made it all the way to the end of this book. Great job on reading all the way through! I hope you had a good time, learned what the science of habits has uncovered, and, most importantly, picked up some powerful strategies to try out for yourself.

Because that's what it all comes down to, really. You can read all the books in the world and get fantastic insights and ideas, but they won't create any change unless you actually apply them to your own life.

That's why I encourage you to adopt the "scientist and subject" mindset I wrote about at the very beginning of this book. Try the strategies, view whatever results you get (successful or not) as valuable data, and keep adjusting your approach until you find a way that works for you.

You'll likely find some of the steps in this book very powerful while others are not as helpful. That's perfectly fine and to be expected. While all of the steps in this book are based on successful scientific findings, that doesn't mean they will all fit your unique psychology. Focus on what works and forget about the rest. Or better yet, teach it to others who are struggling with their habits. A strategy that's a complete dud for you can turn out to be very effective for someone else.

Also, remember that this isn't about hitting some arbitrary number of days when your habit will somehow become completely automatic so you can just sit back and slack off. Rather, it's about changing your identity and your mindset in how you approach your life.

Challenge yourself with big, audacious goals but always be very aware that it's your ability to show up every day and take action that will get you there.

They say Rome wasn't built in a day. But they were laying bricks every hour. All you need to worry about is laying that next brick. If you do that, if you can commit to the process and refuse to quit, you will inevitably create any change you want in your life.

Grab Your Free Workbook

If you haven't already, now is the time to download the *The Habit Blueprint Workbook*, pick a habit you'd like to create for yourself, and start working your way through the steps.

https://patrikedblad.com/the-habit-blueprint-book-bonuses

Oh, and don't hesitate to drop me a message if you have any thoughts, questions, or feedback (or just want to say hi). I love hearing from readers, and I'll get back to you as soon as I can.

Here's to your new habit!

Your friend and habit coach,

Get Your Next Blueprint

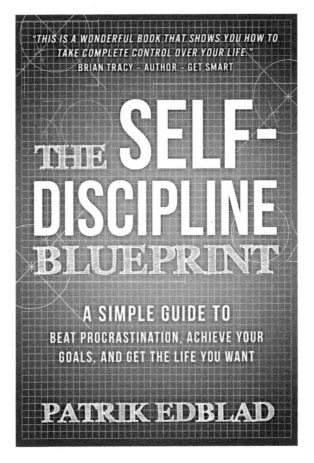

Go Here to Grab *The Self-Discipline Blueprint*:

https://patrikedblad.com/books/the-self-discipline-blueprint

The Self-Discipline Blueprint is the complete step-by-step guide to achieve anything you set your mind to. Each chapter covers practical and efficient ways to develop relentless self-discipline, all backed by research. Inside the book, you'll discover:

- the four fundamental keystone habits of self-discipline;
- how to establish your mission in life using The Hedgehog Concept;
- how to find your unique "why" using The Golden Circle;

- how to get laser-focused on the right things by defining your Circle of Competence;

- how to biologically reshape your mind and body for success by creating a Winner Effect;

- and much more.

PLUS: The Self-Discipline Blueprint Workbook—a bonus resource you can use to put everything you learn into immediate action.

Take the next step in your self-actualization journey right now:

Get *The Self-Discipline Blueprint* today!

Sources

1. Neal, David T., Wendy Wood, and Jeffrey M. Quinn. "Habits—A Repeat Performance." *Current Directions in Psychological Science* 15, no. 4 (2006): 198–202. web.archive.org/web/20110526144503/ http:/dornsife.usc.edu/wendywood/research/documents/Neal. Wood.Quinn.2006.pdf.

2. "New Years Resolutions Statistics." Statistic Brain. Accessed October 12, 2016. www.statisticbrain.com/new-years-resolution-statistics/.

3. Patterson, Kerry, Joseph Grenny, David Maxfield, Ron McMillan, and Al Switzler. *Change Anything: The New Science of Personal Success*. New York: Grand Central Publishing, 2011. Kindle edition.

4. Duhigg, Charles. "How Habits Work." Charles Duhigg. Accessed 10/12/2016. charlesduhigg.com/how-habits-work/.

5. Duhigg, Charles. The Power of Habit: Why We Do What We Do in Life. New York: Random House, 2014. Kindle edition.

6. Danziger, Shai, Jonathan Levav, and Liora Avnaim-Pesso. "Extraneous Factors in Judicial Decision." *Proceedings of the National Academy of Sciences of the United States of America* 108, no. 17 (2011): 6889–6892. doi:10.1073/pnas.1018033108.

7. Baumeister, Roy F. "Ego Depletion and Self-Control Failure: An Energy Model of the Self's Executive Function." *Self and Identity* 1 (2002): 129–136. www.communicationcache.com/ uploads/1/0/8/8/10887248/ego_depletion_and_self-control_ failure-_an_energy_model_of_the_sels_executive_function.pdf.

8. Babauta, Leo. "The Four Habits that Form Habits." *Zen Habits* (blog). Published February 13, 2013. zenhabits.net/habitses/.

9. Dean, Jeremy. "The Zeigarnik Effect." *PsyBlog* (blog). Published February 8, 2011. www.spring.org.uk/2011/02/the-zeigarnik-effect.php.

10. Trapani, Gina. "Jerry Seinfeld's Productivity Secret." Lifehacker. Published July 24, 2007. lifehacker.com/281626/jerry-seinfelds-productivity-secret.

11. Arkes, Hal, and Catherine Blumer. "The Psychology of Sunk Cost." Organizational Behavior and Human Decision Processes 35, no. 1 (1985): 124–140. doi:10.1016/0749-5978(85)90049-4

12. Gollwitzer, Peter M. "Implementation Intentions: Strong Effects of Simple Plans." *American Psychologist* 54, no. 7 (1999): 493–503. www.psych.nyu.edu/gollwitzer/99Goll_ImpInt.pdf.

13. Scott, S. J. *Habit Stacking: 97 Small Life Changes That Take Five Minutes or Less.* N.p.: Oldtown Publishing, 2014.

14. Buehler, Roger, Dale Griffin, and Michael Ross. "Exploring the 'Planning Fallacy': Why People Underestimate Their Task Completion Times." *Journal of Personality and Social Psychology* 67, no. 3 (1994): 366–381. web.mit.edu/curhan/www/docs/Articles/biases/67_J_Personality_and_Social_Psychology_366,_1994.pdf.

15. Vohs, Kathleen D., Brandon J. Schmeichel, Noelle M. Nelson, Roy F. Baumeister, Jean M. Twenge, Dianne M. Tice. "Making Choices Impairs Subsequent Self-Control: A Limited-Resource Account of Decision Making, Self-Regulation, and Active Initiative." *Journal of Personality and Social Psychology* 94, no. 5 (2008): 883–898. doi:10.1037/0022-3514.94.5.883.

16. Artino, Anthony R. "Self-Reinforcement." In *Encyclopedia of Child Behavior and Development.* Springer US, 2011. Accessed 10/12/2016. doi:10.1007/978-0-387-79061-9_2560.

17. McLeod, Saul. "Skinner – Operant Conditioning." Simply Psychology. Last modified 2015. www.simplypsychology.org/operant-conditioning.html.

18. Carney, Dana R., Amy J. C. Cuddy, and Andy J. Yap. "Power Posing: Brief Nonverbal Displays Affect Neuroendocrine Levels and Risk Tolerance." *Psychological Science* 21, no. 10 (2010): 1363–1368. doi:10.1177/0956797610383437.

19. Marzoli, Daniele, Mariagrazia Custodero, Alessandra Pagliara, and Luca Tommasi. "Sun-Induced Frowning Fosters Aggressive Feelings." *Cognition and Emotion* 27, no. 8 (2013): 1513–1521. dx.doi.org/10.1080/02699931.2013.801338.

20. Stel, Mariëlle, Eric van Dijk, Pamela K. Smith, Wilco W. van Dijk, and Farah M. Djalal. "Lowering the Pitch of Your Voice Makes You Feel More Powerful and Think More Abstractly." *Social Psychological and Personality Science* 3, no. 4 (2012): 497–502. doi:10.1177/1948550611427610.

21. Fogg, BJ. "BJ's Note: September 23, 2012 3:53 pm PST." Welcome to My Sandbox (blog). Published September 23, 2012. tinyhabits. com/sandbox/.

22. Fogg, BJ. "Ways to Celebrate Tiny Successes." SlideShare slideshow. Published August 29, 2012. www.slideshare.net/tinyhabits/ dr-bj-fogg-ways-to-celebrate-tiny-successes.

23. Fiore, Neil. *The Now Habit: A Strategic Program for Overcoming Procrastination and Enjoying Guilt-Free Play.* New York: TarcherPerigree, 2007. Kindle edition.

24. Ferreri, Summer. "Token Economy." In *Encyclopedia of Autism Spectrum Disorders.* Springer New York, 2013. Accessed 10/12/2016. doi:10.1007/978-1-4419-1698-3_198.

25. Henry, Alan. "Productivity 101: A Primer to the Pomodoro Technique." Lifehacker. Published July 2, 2014. lifehacker.com/productivity-101- a-primer-to-the-pomodoro-technique-1598992730

26. Lally, Phillippa, Cornelia H. M. van Jaarsveld, Henry W. W. Potts, and Jane Wardle. "How Habits Are Formed: Modelling Habit Formation in the Real World." *European Journal of Social Psychology* 40, no. 6 (2010): 998–1009. doi:10.1002/ejsp.674.

27. Schnoll, Roseanne, and Barry Zimmerman. "Self-Regulation Training Enhances Dietary Self-Efficacy and Dietary Fiber Consumption." *Journal of the American Dietetic Association* 101, no. 9 (2001): 1006–1011. doi:10.1016/S0002-8223(01)00249-8.

28. Robins, Lee N., John E. Helzer, Michie Hesselbrock, and Eric Wish. "Vietnam Veterans Three Years after Vietnam: How Our Study Changed Our View of Heroin." *American Journal on Addictions* 19, no. 3 (2010): 203–211. Doi:10.1111/j.1521-0391.2010.00046.x.

29. Csikszentmihalyi, Mihaly. *Finding Flow: The Psychology of Engagement with Everyday Life.* New York: Basic Books, 2007. Kindle edition.

30. Thorndike, Anne, Lillian Sonnenberg, Jason Riis, Susan Barraclough, and Douglas Levey. "A 2 Phase Labeling and Choice Architecture Intervention to Improve Healthy Food and Beverage Choices." *American Journal of Public Health* 102, no. 4 (2012): 584. doi:10.2105/AJPH.2011.300391.

31. Sewell, William H., and Vimal P. Shah. "Parents' Education and Children's Educational Aspirations and Achievements." *American Psychological Review* 33, no. 2 (1968): 191–209. www.ssc.wisc.edu/wlsresearch/publications/files/public/Sewell-Shah_Parents.Education.C.E.A.A.pdf.

32. Aarts, Henk, Peter M. Gollwitzer, and Ran R. Hassin. "Goal Contagion: Perceiving Is for Pursuing." *Journal of Personality and Social Psychology* 87, no. 1 (2004): 23–37. www.goallab.nl/publications/documents/Aarts,%20Gollwitzer,%20Hassin%20(2004)%20-%20goal%20contagion.pdf.

33. Christakis, Nicholas, and James Fowler. "The Spread of Obesity in a Large Social Network Over 32 Years." *New England Journal of Medicine* 357, no. 4 (2007): Epub. doi:10.1056/NEJMsa066082.

34. Doherty, R. William, Lisa Orimoto, Theodore M. Singelis, Elaine Hatfield, and Janine Hebb. "Emotional Contagion: Gender and Occupational Differences." *Psychology of Women Quarterly* 19 (1995): 355–371. www2.hawaii.edu/~elaineh/91.pdf.

35. Giné, Xavier, Dean Karlan, and Jonathan Zinman. "Put Your Money Where Your Butt Is: A Commitment Contract for Smoking Cessation." *American Economic Journal: Applied Economics* 2 (2010): 213–235. karlan.yale.edu/sites/default/files/app2e22e42e213.pdf.

36. McCarney, Rob, James Warner, Steve Iliffe, Robbert van Haselen, Mark Griffin, and Peter Fisher. "The Hawthorne Effect: A Randomised, Controlled Trial." *BMC Medical Research Methodology* 7, no. 30 (2007). doi:10.1186/1471-2288-7-30.

37. Read, Daniel, and Barbara van Leeuwen. "Predicting Hunger: The Effects of Appetite and Delay on Choice." *Organizational Behavior and Human Decision Processes* 76, no. 2 (1998): 189–205. doi:10.1006/obhd.1998.2803.

38. Rubin, Gretchen. *Better than Before: Mastering the Habits of Our Everyday Lives.* London: Two Roads, 2015. Kindle edition.

39. Polivy, Janet, C. Peter Herman, and Rajbir Deo. "Getting a Bigger Slice of the Pie: Effects on Eating and Emotion in Restrained and Unrestrained Eaters." *Appetite* 55, no. 3 (2010): 426–430. doi:dx.doi.org/10.1016/j.appet.2010.07.015.

40. Lally, van Jaarsveld, Potts, and Wardle. "How Habits Are Formed." *European Journal of Social Psychology* 40, no. 6 (2010): 998–1009. doi:10.1002/ejsp.674.

41. Wohl, Michael J. A., Timothy A. Pychyl, and Shannon H. Bennett. "I Forgive Myself, Now I Can Study: How Self-Forgiveness for Procrastinating Can Reduce Future Procrastination." *Personality and Individual Differences* 48, no. 7 (2010): 803–808. doi: dx.doi.org/10.1016/j.paid.2010.01.029.

Made in the USA
Columbia, SC
14 March 2022

57622753R00039